OBJECTIVE
KET
for Schools

Practice Test Booklet
WITHOUT ANSWERS

Annette Capel
Wendy Sharp

CAMBRIDGE
UNIVERSITY PRESS

CAMBRIDGE UNIVERSITY PRESS
Cambridge, New York, Melbourne, Madrid, Cape Town, Singapore,
São Paulo, Delhi, Dubai, Tokyo, Mexico City

Cambridge University Press
The Edinburgh Building, Cambridge CB2 8RU, UK

www.cambridge.org
Information on this title: www.cambridge.org/9780521178976

© Cambridge University Press 2009

First published 2009
Reprinted 2010

Printed in the United Kingdom by Latimer Trend

A catalogue record for this publication is available from the British Library

ISBN 978-0-521-17897-6 Practice Test Booklet without answers
ISBN 978-0-521-74461-4 Practice Test Booklet with answers with Audio CD
ISBN 978-0-521-74466-9 Pack
ISBN 978-0-521-54149-7 Student's Book
ISBN 978-0-521-54150-3 Teacher's Book
ISBN 978-0-521-54151-0 Cassette Set
ISBN 978-0-521-54152-7 Audio CD Set
ISBN 978-0-521-61994-3 Workbook
ISBN 978-0-521-61995-0 Workbook with Answers

Contents

Acknowledgements

The authors and publishers acknowledge the following sources of copyright material and are grateful for the permissions granted. While every effort has been made, it has not always been possible to identify the sources of all the material used, or to trace all copyright holders. If any omissions are brought to our notice, we will be happy to include the appropriate acknowledgements on reprinting.

Cambridge ESOL for the table on page 5 produced with reference to ALTE Can Do statements. Copyright © UCLES 2008; First news for the adapted text on page 34 'Youngest climber scales Kilimanjaro' from *First News* 9–15 May 2008. Copyright © First News 2008; Irish Independent for adapted text and photo on page 34 '10-year-old reaches Kilimanjaro' from The *Irish Independent* 6 May 2008. Copyright © Irish Independent 2008.

Artwork acknowledgements
Illustrations by John Batten.

Photo acknowledgements
iStockphoto.com/Dan Rowley p7, Photolibrary Group p10, Alex Segre/Alamy p31, First News p34, iStockphoto.com/Peter Engelsted Jonasen p36.

Author acknowledgements
The authors would like to thank Sara Bennett and Laila Friese for their editorial support, and Mike Cryer and John Park of eMC Design for their design solutions.

Introduction

This booklet contains two complete practice tests for the University of Cambridge ESOL Examinations Key English Test for Schools. The tests cover topics typically included in the exam and also target the content of *Objective KET* Student's Book. Students can use these tests on their own or with a teacher.

KET for Schools is a new version of the KET exam for candidates between the ages of 11 and 14. KET for Schools has the same format and task types as KET, and the level of the two versions is identical, but the content and topics are dealt with in ways which reflect the experiences and interests of younger candidates.

KET is at level A2 of the Council of Europe Common European Framework of Reference for Languages. The following 'Can Do' statements show what language learners at KET (A2) level are generally able to do.

Typical abilities	Listening and Speaking	Reading and Writing
Overall general ability	CAN understand simple questions and instructions. CAN express simple opinions or requirements in a familiar context.	CAN understand straightforward information within a known area. CAN complete forms and write short, simple letters or postcards related to personal information.
Social and Leisure	CAN have short conversations with friends about interesting topics. CAN make simple plans with people, such as what to do, where to go, and when to meet. CAN express likes and dislikes in familiar contexts using simple language.	CAN understand short, simple messages from people who share his/her interest, for example emails, postcards or short letters from pen friends.
School and Study	CAN understand basic instructions on class times, dates, and room numbers. CAN ask the person to repeat what they said, when he/she does not understand something. CAN express simple opinions using expressions such as 'I don't agree'.	CAN understand the general meaning of a simplified textbook or story, reading very slowly CAN write about his/her daily life in simple phrases and sentences, for example family, school, hobbies, holidays, likes and dislikes.

The KET examination is one of the Cambridge ESOL Main Suite examinations, which cover CEFR levels A2 to C2. The following table* demonstrates how the five Main Suite examinations correlate to the CEFR levels.

CPE	C2 Mastery
CAE	C1 Effective proficiency
FCE	B2 Vantage
PET	B1 Threshold
KET	A2 Waystage

The KET / KET for Schools examination is a basic qualification in English and can also be a first step for those wishing to progress towards the Preliminary English Test (PET / PET for Schools) and other Cambridge ESOL examinations.

Good luck with these tests, and with KET for Schools!

* © UCLES 2008, produced with reference to ALTE Can Do statements

Test 1

Paper 1 (1 hour 10 minutes)

Reading and Writing Part 1

Questions 1 – 5

Which notice **(A – H)** says this **(1 – 5)**?
For questions **1 – 5**, mark the correct letter **A – H** on your answer sheet.

Example:

0   One of our meals costs less at the moment.

Answer:

0	A	B	C	D	E	F	G	H
	☐	☐	☐	■	☐	☐	☐	☐

---

1   Some of the food that is sold here comes from the countryside.

2   If you order a certain dish today, we will give you something extra.

3   You can try a new lunch menu at this place.

4   Someone will show you to your table.

5   If you eat here, you can use a computer without paying.

A   PEPE'S PIZZAHOUSE
This week only: free salad with every pizza

B   Please wait here for a seat in our restaurant

C   INTERNET CAFÉ
1 hour free online with food menu orders

D   TODAY'S SPECIAL: Fish and chips half normal price

E   CARLA'S CAFÉ
We now have different Spanish dishes (12–3pm)

F   YOUR SPECIAL SANDWICH?
The best idea wins a free lunch!

G   ALL OUR ICE CREAM IS MADE ON OUR FARM

H   INDIAN FOOD EVENING
BOOK YOUR TABLE ONLINE TODAY!

www.curryprince.com

Reading and Writing Part 2

Questions 6 – 10

Read the sentences about hippos.
Choose the best word **(A, B** or **C)** for each space.
For questions **6 – 10**, mark **A**, **B** or **C** on your answer sheet.

Example:

0   The hippopotamus is more usually .... as the hippo.

  A   known   **B**   called   **C**   noted

Answer:

0	A	B	C
	■	☐	☐

---

6   Hippos .... in Africa in groups of between 5 and 30.

  A   stay   **B**   live   **C**   keep

7   Hippos spend most of the .... resting in rivers or lakes.

  A   hour   **B**   age   **C**   day

8   At night, hippos .... out of the water to eat plants on land.

  A   follow   **B**   come   **C**   leave

9   A hippo only has .... legs but it can still run faster than a man.

  A   short   **B**   round   **C**   low

10   Baby hippos are born under water and they can swim .... after they are born.

  A   suddenly   **B**   actually   **C**   immediately

Reading and Writing Part 3

Questions 11 – 15

Complete the five conversations.
For questions **11 – 15**, mark **A**, **B** or **C** on your answer sheet.

Example:

0

What's she like?

A She's tall and thin.

B She likes bananas.

C She doesn't want to.

Answer: **0** A B C

---

11 Why can't you go to Sam's match?

    A It isn't mine.

    B We're away.

    C Of course.

12 I haven't got the right money for the drinks machine.

    A It's a lovely drink.

    B It's over there, isn't it?

    C It's OK, it gives change.

13 Look out – that plastic bag's broken!

    A Did you see it?

    B Can I carry yours?

    C Have you got another?

14 Text me before you leave.

    A What's the number?

    B When did you arrive?

    C Who will send them?

15 Would you like some more pizza?

    A I like that.

    B I'm full, thanks.

    C I can't eat pizza.

Questions 16 – 20

Complete the conversation between two friends.
What does Olga say to Jamie?
For questions **16 – 20**, mark the correct letter **A – H** on your answer sheet.

Example:

Jamie: Olga, what are you bringing to the class party tomorrow?

Olga: **0** ......**B**......   Answer: | **0** | A B C D E F G H |

Jamie: I haven't done anything about it yet!

Olga: **16** ....

Jamie: The teachers are getting all the drinks, I think.

Olga: **17** ....

Jamie: Everyone takes those! Shall I buy some fruit?

Olga: **18** ....

Jamie: I'm not sure. Perhaps some apples and pears?

Olga: **19** ....

Jamie: OK, I'll get a big pineapple in the market instead.

Olga: **20** ....

Jamie: Yeah. I'll do that at home.

A Good idea! What kinds?

B I've made a big chocolate cake. How about you?

C Perhaps they'll get enough.

D That's nice of them. Well, bring some biscuits then.

E They're really expensive, you know.

F What a surprise! Why don't you buy some juice?

G That sounds better. You can cut it into pieces.

H You can do that this afternoon.

Reading and Writing Part 4

Questions 21 – 27

Read the article about a school trip to Japan and then answer the questions.
For questions **21 – 27**, mark **A**, **B** or **C** on your answer sheet.

Matt's trip to Japan

I started learning Japanese four years ago and, two years later, I visited Japan for three weeks with other classmates. We flew to Osaka and I was surprised at how big Osaka Airport was. We stayed one night on the 10th floor of a new building and then took a really quick train to Hiroshima – that journey was an even bigger surprise!

We went to Kyoto next. I lost my camera there so I drew lots of the places I saw. In Kyoto, we stayed at Utano Youth Hostel. It had nice rooms for eight, and some warm, helpful people worked there.

When we arrived at the school in Yokohama, all the students welcomed us in the hall with songs and music. Then we were shown around and my homestay family collected me. They gave me great food and made me use my Japanese every day, so it got much better. They drove me around too.

I did many activities at the school, like Japanese drumming and sport. I tried Japanese writing but it wasn't easy. The volleyball team let me practise with them, which was fun.

It rained a lot during our last days in Tokyo but that wasn't a problem. The shops were great but what I won't forget is the number of people everywhere. I'm sure I'll go back one day.

Example:

0   Matt went to Japan

     A   two years ago.

     B   three years ago.

     C   four years ago.

Answer: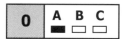

---

21   At the beginning of his trip, what surprised Matt the most?

     A   the tall building

     B   the fast train

     C   the large airport

22   How did Matt spend his time in Kyoto?

     A   making notes

     B   taking photos

     C   drawing pictures

23   What does Matt say about Utano?

     A   It had friendly staff.

     B   It had single rooms.

     C   It had good heating.

24   At the school in Yokohama, the first thing Matt did was to

     A   meet his Japanese family.

     B   listen to a concert.

     C   go on a tour.

25   Matt's Japanese family helped him

     A   to improve his Japanese.

     B   to travel to the school.

     C   to cook Japanese food.

26   Which activity did Matt find hard?

     A   drumming

     B   volleyball

     C   writing

27   What will Matt always remember about Tokyo?

     A   the shops

     B   the crowds

     C   the weather

Reading and Writing Part 5

Questions 28 – 35

Read the article about surfing clothes.
Choose the best word (**A**, **B** or **C**) for each space.
For questions **28 – 35**, mark **A**, **B** or **C** on your answer sheet.

Clothes for board sports

Do you like **(0)** .... go surfing, windsurfing or skateboarding? **(28)** .... you do, then you may **(29)** .... enjoy choosing clothes for your sport.

Board shorts and T-shirts are the **(30)** .... popular clothes among surfers. The T-shirts that surfers wear often have unusual messages on them. Board shorts come in **(31)** .... different colours and are very comfortable. They look good **(32)** .... well!

For the last ten years, the companies that **(33)** .... clothes for board sports have had great success. **(34)** .... clothes have stayed in fashion because they are part of a special way of life to do with sea, sun and sport.

So, wearing these clothes, you **(35)** .... dream of the beach even sitting in your room at home!

Example:

0	**A**	to	**B**	of	**C**	at	*Answer:*	

0	A	B	C
	■	☐	☐

---

28 **A** When **B** And **C** If

29 **A** both **B** also **C** too

30 **A** more **B** much **C** most

31 **A** many **B** lot **C** any

32 **A** like **B** by **C** as

33 **A** make **B** makes **C** making

34 **A** Its **B** Their **C** His

35 **A** need **B** shall **C** can

Reading and Writing Part 6

Questions 36 – 40

Read the descriptions of some words about shopping.
What is the word for each one?
The first letter is already there. There is one space for each other letter in the word.
For questions **36 – 40**, write the words on your answer sheet.

Example:

0   This person works in a shop and is there to help you.   **a** _ _ _ _ _ _ _ _

Answer: | **0** | *assistant* |

---

36   If you need medicine, you should go to this shop.   **c** _ _ _ _ _ _

37   You can buy your favourite magazine here.   **n** _ _ _ _ _ _ _ _

38   This place is often outside and people sell fresh vegetables there.   **m** _ _ _ _ _

39   If you buy something from a shop, you are one of these.   **c** _ _ _ _ _ _ _ _

40   You can visit this if you want to shop online.   **w** _ _ _ _ _ _

Reading and Writing Part 7

Questions 41 – 50

Complete the messages left on the internet by two students.
Write ONE word for each space.
For questions **41 – 50**, write the words on your answer sheet.

Example: | **0** | in |

Hi, I'm Carolina and I live **(0)** .... Brazil. Music is really important **(41)** .... most Brazilians. Do people in **(42)** .... countries feel the same way **(43)** .... music? How many people out there play **(44)** .... instrument? I love to play the drums but I'm **(45)** .... very good yet!

Hi, I'm Juan and I come **(46)** .... the south of Spain. I love **(47)** .... kind of music! My favourite kind is the wonderful Spanish guitar music **(48)** .... is called flamenco. It's very popular because **(49)** .... of Spanish bands include flamenco in their songs. I'm learning to play the guitar myself but **(50)** .... is electric!

Reading and Writing Part 8

Questions 51 – 55

Read the advertisement and the email.
Fill in the information in Tom's notes.
For questions **51 – 55**, write the information on your answer sheet.

BATMAN

AT THE ODEON CINEMA NEXT WEEKEND

**See all the Batman and
Catwoman films ever made!**

All day Saturday & Sunday,
first film starts at 10.15 a.m.

Weekend ticket £28.90
(One day only £16.30)

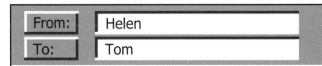

| From: | Helen |
| To: | Tom |

Hi Tom

Great you can see the Batman movies. I'm busy on Sunday so let's go on the other day. Instead of meeting at the station, why not wait for me inside the café at 9.45? Please remember my dictionary. I'll bring snacks for later!

Helen

Tom's notes
Batman films

Cinema: Odeon

Day: **51** [ ]

Time to meet Helen: **52** [a.m.]

Where to meet Helen: **53** [ ]

Price of my ticket: **54** [£]

What to bring: **55** [ ]

Reading and Writing Part 9

Question 56

You are going to watch an international football match on television tonight.
Write an email to your English friend Alex.

Tell Alex:

- **what TV channel** the match will be on

- **which countries** will play in the match

- **why** you think the match will be good.

Write **25 – 35** words.
Write the email on your answer sheet.

Paper 2 (approximately 30 minutes including 8 minutes' transfer time)

Listening Part 1

Questions 1 – 5

You will hear five short conversations.
You will hear each conversation twice.
There is one question for each conversation.
For each question, choose the right answer **(A**, **B** or **C)**.

Example: How many people belong to the swimming club?

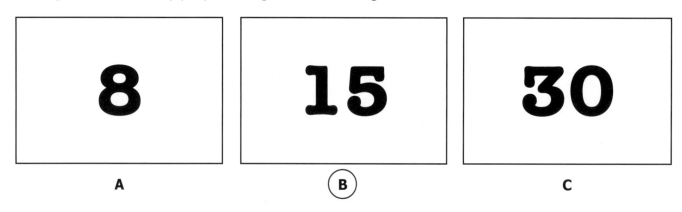

A   **B**   **C**

---

1   Which DVD will the friends watch today?

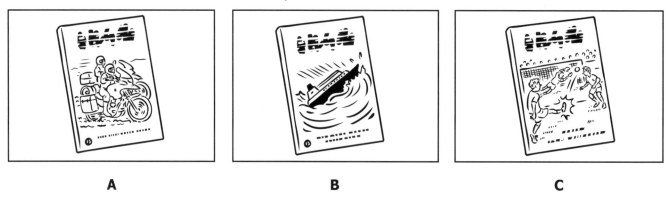

A   **B**   **C**

2   What is Rita going to wear to the party?

A   **B**   **C**

3   Which vegetables does Alex need to buy for his soup?

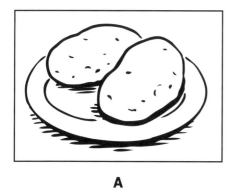

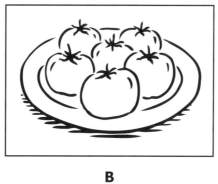

A   **B**   **C**

4   What did Katy do last Saturday?

A   **B**   **C**

5   What needs changing in the boy's bedroom?

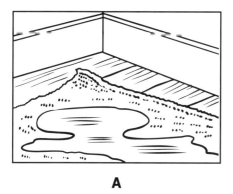

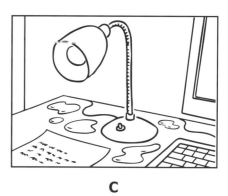

A   **B**   **C**

Listening Part 2

Questions 6 – 10

Listen to Anna telling her friend, Tom, about her things from different countries.
Which country does each thing come from?
For questions **6 – 10**, write a letter **A – H** next to each country.
You will hear the conversation twice.

Example:

0   The USA | **G** |

COUNTRIES		**THINGS**
6 Australia		**A** bowl
7 Switzerland		**B** box
8 Canada		**C** guitar
9 Brazil		**D** mirror
10 China		**E** pen
		F poster
		G skateboard
		H toy animal

Listening Part 3

Questions 11 – 15

Listen to James talking to a friend about a school barbecue.
For each question, choose the right answer **(A**, **B** or **C)**.
You will hear the conversation twice.

Example:

0   Which day is the barbecue?

    A   Wednesday

    (B)   Thursday

    C   Saturday

---

11   The barbecue will begin at

    A   6.30.

    B   7.15.

    C   7.45.

12   What music will the band play?

    A   piano

    B   rock

    C   hip hop

13   What meat will James take for the barbecue?

    A   steak

    B   burgers

    C   chicken

14   Which drink is James going to get?

    A   lemonade

    B   fruit juice

    C   mineral water

15   This year, the barbecue will be

    A   on the sports field.

    B   by the pool.

    C   in the garden.

Listening Part 4

Questions 16 – 20

You will hear a boy, Ben, talking to a friend about a school trip to a zoo.
Listen and complete each question.
You will hear the conversation twice.

School Trip to Bristol Zoo

Date of trip: 24 February

Time coach will leave: **(16)** .... a.m.

Total cost of trip: **(17)** £ ....

Give money to: **(18)** M r s ....

What to bring for project: **(19)** ....

What else to bring: **(20)** ....

Listening Part 5

Questions 21 – 25

You will hear a man on the radio talking about a sale at a school.
Listen and complete each question.
You will hear the information twice.

Bridge Street School Sale

Day of sale: $\quad$ Saturday

Sale ends at: $\quad$ **(21)** .... p.m.

Entry price for a teenager: $\quad$ **(22)** £ ....

Place where games will be: $\quad$ **(23)** ....

Person opening the sale: $\quad$ a famous
$\quad$ **(24)** ....

School office phone number: $\quad$ **(25)** ....

Paper 3
About the Speaking test

Part 1 (5 – 6 minutes)

In this part, the examiner asks you questions to find out personal information, such as your surname, where you are from, where you live and about your family. You may also need to answer questions about your daily life, for example your school or hobbies.

Part 2 (3 – 4 minutes)

In this part, you and your partner(s) talk together. You ask and answer questions to find out information. The examiner will give you a card with some information on it. The examiner will give your partner another card with some words to help them make questions. Your partner will ask you questions, and you need to read the information on your card to answer the questions. You will then change roles with your partner.

Note: The visual materials for Part 2 are on pages 26 and 27.

Visual materials for Paper 3

Tests 1 and 2

1A

Happy Days Shopping Centre

Open 9 a.m. – 22.30 p.m. Monday to Saturday (11 a.m. – 5 p.m. Sunday)

More than 120 shops, including Linley's department store, bookshops, clothes shops, sports shops and many more

Cafés and restaurants on every floor

Free car park

1C

School band competition

Are you in a rock, pop or hip hop band?
Then this competition is for you!

Friday 19 June
(1 p.m. – 4 p.m. in the school hall)

Prize £100

To play in the competition, tell Miss White <u>by Friday 12 June</u>

1B

SHOPPING CENTRE

- how / big?

- kind / shops?

- when / open?

- car park?

- where / eat?

1D

MUSIC COMPETITION

- date / competition?

- where / competition?

- what time / start?

- which / bands?

- how much / prize?

2A

School Winter Sports Trip

Trip to Switzerland for skiing and skating – £550

8–16 February

Flying from Manchester airport and staying in a hotel.

Pocket money is not included.

2C

Photo competition

for anyone 11–15 years old

Take a photo of your school!

Send your photo before 2nd July to
14 Bridge Street
Wilton

**Prize:
£600 digital camera**

2B

TRIP

- where / go?

- when / leave

- how / travel?

- price?

- what / take?

2D

COMPETITION

- what / do?

- how / old?

- where / send?

- when / send?

- what / win?

Test 2
Paper 1 (1 hour 10 minutes)
Reading and Writing Part 1

Questions 1 – 5

Which notice **(A – H)** says this **(1 – 5)**?
For questions **1 – 5**, mark the correct letter **A – H** on your answer sheet.

Example:

0   You must not leave this on.

Answer:

---

1   Use the correct money if you want to buy something from here.

2   These are much cheaper to buy now.

3   Don't forget to take these things.

4   You can't go to this if you haven't already booked.

5   A member of staff will help you with this.

A

> Ask a teacher if there's a problem with a laptop

B

> Mr Duncan will teach class 5A next term

C

> Football match – all seats now full

D

> **Drinks machine: No change given**

E

> **Sale**
> *All mobiles half price or less today*

F

> Text 'NOW' for up to 100 free texts

G

> *Remember to bring a pen and notebook on the school trip*

H

> **Turn computer off after use**

Reading and Writing Part 2

Questions 6 – 10

Read the sentences about buying a computer.
Choose the best word (**A**, **B** or **C**) for each space.
For questions **6 – 10**, mark **A**, **B** or **C** on your answer sheet.

Example:

0   Last Saturday, Daniel .... the afternoon shopping with his dad.

A went	**B** spent	**C** came	*Answer:*	0 A ☐ B ■ C ☐

---

6   Daniel's dad wanted to .... Daniel a computer for his birthday.

A   have   **B**   get   **C**   take

7   They saw some really nice computers in the .... of one of the shops.

A   shelf   **B**   table   **C**   window

8   The shop assistant was very .... at helping Daniel choose a computer.

A   excellent   **B**   great   **C**   good

9   Daniel knew what .... of computer he wanted.

A   kind   **B**   present   **C**   idea

10   Daniel can now use his computer to .... his homework.

A   make   **B**   put   **C**   do

Reading and Writing Part 3

Questions 11 – 15

Complete the five conversations.
For questions **11 – 15**, mark **A**, **B** or **C** on your answer sheet.

Example:

0

What's she like?

A She's tall and thin.

B She likes bananas.

C She doesn't want to.

Answer: **0** ■A ☐B ☐C

---

11 How much money do you have?

    A I can have some.

    B I'm not sure.

    C Yes, I have.

12 I live near the station.

    A Do you?

    B Will you?

    C Should you?

13 He missed the bus home.

    A Oh dear!

    B Come on!

    C Bye-bye!

14 Are you hurt?

    A No, it isn't.

    B No, I'm alright.

    C Not bad.

15 How long have you played football?

    A Three years ago.

    B Since three years.

    C For three years.

Questions 16 − 20

Complete the telephone conversation between two friends.
What does Carmen say to Magda?
For questions **16 − 20**, mark the correct letter **A − H** on your answer sheet.

Example:

Magda: Hi, Carmen. It's Magda.

Carmen: **0** ....**D**........   *Answer:* | **0** | A B C D E F G H |

Magda: That's OK. I'm ringing about the school camping trip we're going on.

Carmen: **16** ....

Magda: Almost, but I haven't got a tent I can use.

Carmen: **17** ....

Magda: That's great. What are you putting your things in?

Carmen: **18** ....

Magda: OK, I have one of those. They said on TV that the weather's going to be hot.

Carmen: **19** ....

Magda: Don't forget to pack a camera and your mobile.

Carmen: **20** ....

Magda: Me too!

A   Don't worry. My dad has one and he's said we can have it.

B   They're already going.

C   I saw that too.

D   Hi. Sorry I wasn't in earlier.

E   Of course not! I'm so excited!

F   My teacher told us to take a rucksack not a suitcase.

G   It's next week, isn't it? Are you ready yet?

H   I'd like to as well.

Reading and Writing Part 4

Questions 21 – 27

Read the article about climbing Mount Kilimanjaro.
Are sentences **21 – 27** 'Right' **(A)** or 'Wrong' **(B)**?
If there is not enough information to answer 'Right' **(A)** or 'Wrong' **(B)**, choose 'Doesn't say' **(C)**.
For questions **21 – 27**, mark **A**, **B** or **C** on your answer sheet.

10-year-old reaches top of Mount Kilimanjaro

A 10-year-old boy from Ireland has become the youngest European to climb one of the world's highest mountains – Mount Kilimanjaro in Tanzania, Africa. Sean McSharry made the climb with his uncle, Ian McKeever, and a 17-year-old called Harry Moore. Both Ian and Sean have climbed mountains before – Ian has climbed mountains all over the world and Sean got to the top of Ireland's highest mountain when he was nine. Harry joined Sean and Ian after hearing Ian speak about climbing at the college he goes to.

All three practised for the climbing trip five days a week. As well as trying to become fit, Sean had to stop eating sweets and eat lots of green vegetables, which he found very hard. After getting to the top of Kilimanjaro, he phoned his mum. She was very pleased and said she knew he could do it.

Mount Kilimanjaro is 5,899 metres high. The youngest person in the world to climb it, Jordan Romero from California, is seven months younger than Sean. Sean doesn't want to stop climbing mountains and the next one he wants to climb is Mont Blanc, the highest mountain in Western Europe.

Example:

0   Sean's home is in Ireland.

A   Right   **B**   Wrong   **C**   Doesn't say   *Answer:* | 0 | A B C |

---

21   Sean is the first member of his family to climb a mountain.

A   Right   **B**   Wrong   **C**   Doesn't say

22   Ian taught Sean how to climb.

A   Right   **B**   Wrong   **C**   Doesn't say

23   Harry often goes mountain climbing.

A   Right   **B**   Wrong   **C**   Doesn't say

24   Before the trip, Ian, Sean and Harry spent several days each week getting themselves ready.

A   Right   **B**   Wrong   **C**   Doesn't say

25   Sean needed to change what he usually ate.

A   Right   **B**   Wrong   **C**   Doesn't say

26   Sean's mum was unhappy about Sean climbing the mountain.

A   Right   **B**   Wrong   **C**   Doesn't say

27   Sean has plans to climb other mountains.

A   Right   **B**   Wrong   **C**   Doesn't say

Reading and Writing Part 5

Questions 28 – 35

Read the article about a circus family.
Choose the best word (**A**, **B** or **C**) for each space.
For questions **28 – 35**, mark **A**, **B** or **C** on your answer sheet.

I'm in the circus!

My name is Carolina Rizzi and my family **(0)** .... worked
in the circus for over a hundred years. My dad, Tomas Rizzi,
looks after the horses and he rides **(28)** .... in the show.
I'm in the show too, and I ride Fuzz, one of **(29)** ....
smallest horses.

(30) .... the week, I go to school like **(31)** .... children – I go to many different schools
(32) .... the circus is always moving from town to town. At the weekend, I help my dad. We
take the horses into the circus tent and **(33)** .... for the show.

One hour before the show, I change into the special clothes I **(34)** .... to wear. Then I take
Fuzz into the circus tent. I love my life at the circus. **(35)** .... is very exciting!

Example:

0	**A**	has	**B**	is	**C**	was	*Answer:*	0	A B C

28	**A**	theirs	**B**	them	**C**	they

29	**A**	the	**B**	a	**C**	some

30	**A**	Since	**B**	For	**C**	During

31	**A**	another	**B**	other	**C**	others

32	**A**	or	**B**	so	**C**	because

33	**A**	practise	**B**	practised	**C**	practising

34	**A**	need	**B**	must	**C**	should

35	**A**	There	**B**	It	**C**	Here

Reading and Writing Part 6

Questions 36 – 40

Read the descriptions of some words about the journeys that people make.
What is the word for each one?
The first letter is already there. There is one space for each other letter in the word.
For questions **36 – 40**, write the words on your answer sheet.

Example:

0   This has two wheels and is a quick way to get around a town.   **b** _ _ _

Answer:	**0**	*bike*

---

36   This flies but is different from a plane.   **h** _ _ _ _ _ _ _ _ _

37   People travel in this when they are ill.   **a** _ _ _ _ _ _ _ _

38   If you travel across the sea, you go in this.   **s** _ _ _

39   Sometimes there is too much of this on the roads.   **t** _ _ _ _ _ _

40   This will collect you from your home and take you to the station.   **t** _ _ _

Reading and Writing Part 7

Questions 41 – 50

Complete the postcard.
Write ONE word for each space.
For questions **41 – 50**, write the words on your answer sheet.

Example: | **0** | *a t* |

Dear Paola

I've been **(0)** .... this school in New Zealand learning English **(41)** .... two weeks now. We have lessons **(42)** .... morning and in the afternoon we can either go swimming **(43)** .... sailing. **(44)** .... are six other students in my class and I enjoy the class very **(45)** ....

I **(46)** .... staying with a very nice family **(47)** .... live near the school. They have three children – **(48)** .... oldest is the same age as I am, 14. He spends a **(49)** .... of time helping me to practise my English. I'll be home **(50)** .... week, so see you then!

Love

Mia

Reading and Writing Part 8

Questions 51 – 55

Read the advertisement and the email.
Fill in the information on Amanda's form.
For questions **51 – 55**, write the information on your answer sheet.

Adventure Holidays at Southcombe for 11–14-year-olds!

Learn to sail, ride a horse
or have tennis lessons!

All levels

Start dates 11 or 18 July

One week: £389 (two weeks £575)

| From: | Amanda |
| To: | Tullia |

Hi! Let's do this in July. I can only do the second week. Sailing lessons look good – we can both do the beginners' course. Ring me tonight if your parents agree. I have a new mobile no: 077178 93572 but better to ring me at home on 01335 782010.

FORM FOR ADVENTURE HOLIDAY

Name: Amanda Conti

Start date: **51**

Chosen sport: **52**

Level: **53**

Cost: **54**

Home phone number: **55**

Reading and Writing Part 9

Question 56

Read the email from your English friend, Kim.

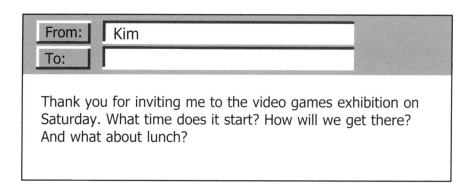

| From: | Kim |
| To: | |

Thank you for inviting me to the video games exhibition on Saturday. What time does it start? How will we get there? And what about lunch?

Write an email to Kim and answer the questions.
Write **25 – 35** words.
Write the email on your answer sheet.

Paper 2 (approximately 30 minutes including 8 minutes' transfer time)

Listening Part 1

Questions 1 – 5

You will hear five short conversations.
You will hear each conversation twice.
There is one question for each conversation.
For each question, choose the right answer (**A**, **B** or **C**).

Example: How many people belong to the swimming club?

A	B	C
8	**15**	**30**

1 What was the weather like on Jane's holiday?

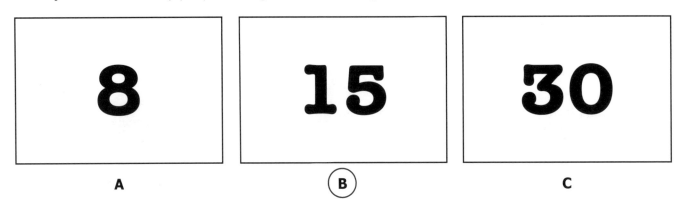

A   B   C

2 Which website is Tom looking at?

A   B   C

3 What time will Ben go to Jenny's party?

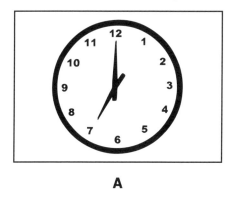 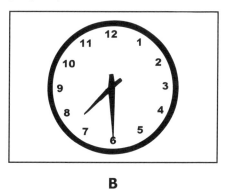 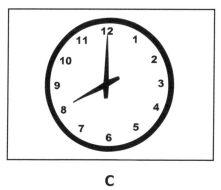

        A   **B**   **C**

4 What hurts Alex the most?

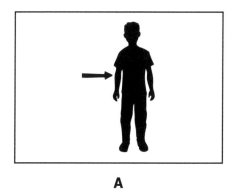 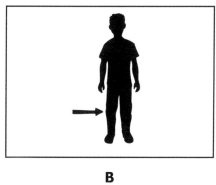 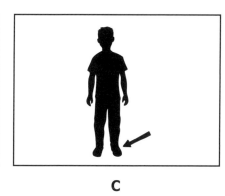

        A   **B**   **C**

5 What did the girl leave in the classroom?

 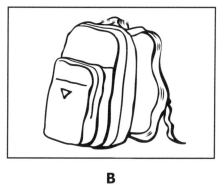 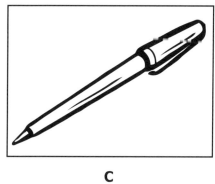

        A   **B**   **C**

Listening Part 2

Questions 6 – 10

Listen to Paul talking to Helen, a new pupil, about the teachers at his school.
Which subject does each teacher teach?
For questions **6 – 10**, write a letter **A – H** next to each teacher.
You will hear the conversation twice.

Example:

0   Mr Matthews   B

TEACHERS   **SUBJECTS**

6   Miss Dunlop   **A**   English

7   Mrs Green   **B**   Geography

                                               C   History

8   Mr Willis

                                               D   Languages

9   Mr Marriot   **E**   Mathematics

10 Miss Donnelly   **F**   Music

                                               G   Science

                                               H   Sport

Listening Part 3

Questions 11 – 15

Listen to Zoe talking to Robert about a mountain bike.
For each question, choose the right answer (**A**, **B** or **C**).
You will hear the conversation twice.

Example:

0   What type of bike does Zoe have?

(**A**)   an FX-13

B   a TX-13

C   a PX-30

---

11   How much was Zoe's bike?

A   £100

B   £150

C   £200

12   Where did Zoe buy her bike?

A   in Finchley

B   in Kilburn

C   in Hammersmith

13   How will Robert get to the bike shop?

A   by bus

B   by motorbike

C   by underground

14   When will Robert go to the bike shop?

A   on Monday

B   on Thursday

C   on Friday

15   What does Zoe tell Robert to buy?

A   a water bottle

B   some lights

C   cycling shorts

Listening Part 4

Questions 16 – 20

You will hear a boy, Chris, asking a friend about joining a sports centre.
Listen and complete each question.
You will hear the conversation twice.

Sports Centre

Student price per month: £18.50

Place of sports centre: opposite the
                                  (16) ....

Take bus number: **(17)** ....

Centre's phone number: **(18)** ....

Go to centre before: **(19)** .... a.m.

Teacher's name: **(20)** Steve ....

Listening Part 5

Questions 21 – 25

You will hear a woman on the radio talking about a new magazine.
Listen and complete each question.
You will hear the information twice.

<u>New Magazine</u>

Name: *Science Now!*

For people studying at: **(21)** ....

Price: **(22)** £ ....

Day magazine is on sale: **(23)** ....

What's free this week: **(24)** ....

Competition prize: **(25)** ....

Paper 3
About the Speaking test

Part 1 (5 – 6 minutes)

In this part, the examiner asks you questions to find out personal information, such as your surname, where you are from, where you live and about your family. You may also need to answer questions about your daily life, for example your school or hobbies.

Part 2 (3 – 4 minutes)

In this part, you and your partner(s) talk together. You ask and answer questions to find out information. The examiner will give you a card with some information on it. The examiner will give your partner another card with some words to help them make questions. Your partner will ask you questions, and you need to read the information on your card to answer the questions. You will then change roles with your partner.

Note: The visual materials for Part 2 are on pages 28 and 29.